Follow Your Heart

21 Days to a Happier, More Fulfilling Life

By
Henri Junttila

Copyright © 2013 by Henri Junttila
All rights reserved.

No part of this book may be reproduced without prior written permission from the author. Reviewers are allowed to quote brief passages in reviews.

Please note that this book is for entertainment purposes only. The views expressed are those of the author alone, and should not be taken as expert instruction or commands. The reader is responsible for his or her own actions.

Table of Contents

Introduction 1
How to Use This Book 3
Day 1: Connect 5
Day 2: Notice Your Reactions 8
Day 3: Do Your Best 12
Day 4: Open Your Heart 15
Day 5: Befriend Fear 19
Day 6: Be Yourself 22
Day 7: Stop Waiting 25
Day 8: Get on the Right Track 28
Day 9: Simplify 31
Day 10: Make Right Decisions 34
Day 11: Unleash Your Inner Artist 37
Day 12: Flow with Life 40

Day 13: Be Still 43

Day 14: Let Your Heart Drive 46

Day 15: Play 49

Day 16: Cut Cords... 52

Day 17: Evolve Your Relationships............ 55

Day 18: Don't Take It Personally 59

Day 19: Allow Abundance........................... 62

Day 20: Take the First Step......................... 65

Day 21: Let Go.. 68

Conclusion... 71

Thank You 73

Connect 74

The Next Step 75

Introduction

Not too long ago, I felt an emptiness in my life. I was making money. I had friends, and everything looked great on the outside, but on the inside, I felt like a piece of me was missing.

I couldn't put my finger on it, but I wasn't following my heart, or following my purpose. I was chasing superficial pleasures. I thought money would make me happy, but it didn't. I thought a relationship would do it, but it didn't. I tried everything, before I finally found the answer.

The answer was to start following my heart. I was skeptical at first, because it seemed like mumbo jumbo to me. But the more I followed my joy, excitement, and passion, the happier I got, and the more fulfilled I felt.

But as I began my journey, I also realized that it wasn't easy. I quickly realized that I had to face my inner demons if I wanted to proceed. I was afraid of what other people might think. I worried about failure. I felt overwhelmed, lost, and frustrated, because I couldn't figure out where my heart was leading me.

It seemed easier to live a logical life, where I'd try to plan everything, but I'd already been down that path. I knew it didn't work. I had nothing to lose, so I started following my heart, and it changed my life. While that may sound cliché, it is what happened.

I'm by no means perfect, and I'll always keep learning, but my life is very different from what it was just a few years ago, and I believe anyone can tap into their heart, purpose, and inner wisdom.

Lasting happiness and fulfillment will never come from something you can achieve or get. It will come from you having the courage to look inside, face your inner demons, and follow your heart. Most people run away from this, but following your purpose is not as scary as it first appears.

When you follow your heart, you connect to the flow of life, which nudges you in a direction you could never have imagined. You no longer try to figure life out. Stress melts away. Happiness expands. You feel more fulfilled.

And the good news is that everyone has access to this, because we all have a heart. The key is to uncover what that process looks like for you, which is why this book is about experimentation. I'm not here to tell you what to do. I'm here to tell you what has worked for me, and what hasn't, so that you can try things out for yourself.

Today, I no longer feel that empty feeling. I don't chase money, and I don't worry as much as I used to. I do work I love, and I wake up excited to be alive. And it's all because I had the courage to start following my heart.

All the answers you need are inside of you. You can tap into your inner wisdom by listening to your heart. So if you're interested in discovering a practical, down-to-earth way to do that, keep reading.

How to Use This Book

This book is divided into 21 chapters, one for each day. Each day focuses on one theme, and one angle from which you can dive deeper into your heart, and increase the happiness in your life.

As with anything I write, my focus is on helping you get real results, not on wowing you with new tips just to impress you. I know I could probably sell more books by going another route, but this is what my heart resonates with, so this is how I write.

You do not have to follow the structure of this book exactly. You'll probably want to start off by reading the book all the way through, while experimenting with the tips that you find interesting. Once you've done that, come back to the days you found interesting, and apply the heart-based action steps.

At the end of each chapter, you'll find a section that gives you three practical tips on how you can implement what you've just learned. These tips takes the guesswork out of connecting to your heart, and help you move forward in tiny, practical steps.

When I talk about following your heart, I'm pointing to the inner wisdom that's always present. We all have an inner GPS that is waiting to guide us. You could call it an inner knowing, instinct, or even intuition. It is a knowing more felt than thought. The label is not as important as what it is pointing to.

Don't just blindly believe what I write, but test it out for yourself. Not everything in this book will be a good fit for you, but it is only through applying what you learn

Follow Your Heart

that you'll discover how to increase the happiness and fulfillment in your life.

Now let's get started.

Day 1: Connect

Connecting to your heart is like tuning into a new radio station. There are many stations to choose from. You may even have grown fond of a few. Some of them are good, while others leave a foul aftertaste.

When you tune into your heart, you become aware of the subtle nudges you get from the wisdom inside you. It doesn't mean you hear a voice in your head—although you could—or that you get stunned by a divine feeling. It's much more subtle than that. It's like a whisper in a noisy room. You won't hear it unless you truly listen.

When you start listening to your heart, it will naturally guide you to the right path. It will help you turn up the happiness and joy in your life. It may not happen all at once, but gradually, the connection becomes stronger.

When we bought a house, I connected to my heart to make the right decision. There was no magic involved. I simply paid attention to the center of my chest. My partner and I knew what we wanted in a house. We spent months looking. At first, the houses we visited just didn't feel right. Some of them looked great in pictures. Some made logical sense. But the moment we stepped into each house, there was something off. My heart wasn't giving me a clear yes.

A clear yes to me feels uplifting, open, and peaceful. That's the signal from my heart that I'm on the right track. As you keep listening to your heart, you'll uncover how your heart communicates.

One day, a new house came on the market. We looked at pictures online, and we almost dismissed it

Follow Your Heart

because it didn't look right. In real life, the house looked completely different, and when we stepped in the door, my heart immediately said yes. But I wasn't in a rush to make a bid. I wanted to sleep on my decision first. Sleeping helps me gain clarity on what exactly my heart is telling me.

As the days passed, the yes became stronger. I still had fears and worries. Buying a house is a big decision, after all. But I also knew that I had what I needed in place. So I followed my heart, made a bid, and we got the house.

You can use your heart to help with any decision in life. It doesn't just help you with big decisions, like buying a house. It's also useful in small decisions, such as what food to buy, who to spend time with, and what books to read.

I've noticed as I've helped people connect to their hearts that the beginning stages are often the most difficult. You aren't sure about what you're doing. And it may feel like you're making things up. After a while, you start trying to force a connection. But all of this is a part of uncovering what works and what doesn't. So go easy on yourself, and expect some struggle.

In short, connecting to your inner wisdom is about learning how your heart communicates with you. If you've never listened to your heart, it may take time to establish a connection, but be patient. Once the connection is there, it'll help steer you towards more joy, purpose, and fulfillment.

Heart-Based Action Steps

Each chapter in this book comes with three practical action steps that you can apply in your life right away. The goal is for you to experiment with what you've learned each day, and see what happens.

Here are the three steps for this chapter:

1. **Become aware of your heart.** The absolute first step is to notice that you have a heart, and to notice that it communicates with you in a certain way. To do this, close your eyes, and imagine bringing your attention from between your eyes to the center of your chest. If you feel like you can't do this, just pretend that you can. There's no right or wrong here.

2. **Welcome anxiety and fear.** If you haven't been aware of your heart for a long time, there may be some anxiety and fear there. If so, let it be. Don't add anything to the feelings, just feel them as best you can. They will pass.

3. **Don't worry if you don't feel anything at first.** Most people won't. Just keep bringing your attention to your heart, and with time, you'll start to learn how your heart communicates. Part of this process is being kind to yourself. There's only so much you can do, so do your best, and let life take care of the rest. Your first step is to keep bringing your attention to the center of your chest, even if nothing magical happens.

Day 2: Notice Your Reactions

You don't see the world exactly as it is, but also as you are. Your experience of life is tinted by your beliefs, past conditioning, and current thoughts. It's impossible to be human and not have a subjective experience of the world. This means that external circumstances are not what's causing you pain or joy, but how you react to them.

For example, when you're standing in line at the store, no one person in that line experiences the same reality as you. Your mood, thoughts, and beliefs all play a role in whether you feel joy or irritation. If someone is holding up the line, you may get irritated, but that doesn't have to mean that you let that irritation take over. If you feel it fully, and welcome it, it slowly dissipates.

I'm not saying you can eliminate your reactions. What I'm saying is that when you become aware of how you react in different situations, you begin to see how you're either creating happiness, or suffering, in your life.

The reason I'm bringing this up is because once you see how you cause struggle in your life, you immediately have more choice. You may not be able to stop or change your reactions right away, but simply becoming aware of them is a step in the right direction.

You didn't come into this world with your reactions. You picked them up from the people around you as you grew up. This conditioning is to a large extent what determines how you live life and how you react to different circumstances.

Follow Your Heart

An old friend of mine was always pessimistic. He was suspicious of people, and he was wary of trying anything new. During my teenage years, we were much alike, and we got along. But as I began following my heart, we started drifting apart. We were even in a minor car crash together while I was living in Spain. The crash wasn't serious. We got a few sprains and bruises. But it pushed my friend deeper into worry, while it made me happy to be alive.

A reaction you may bump into while reading this book is that you can't follow your heart and get your needs met. You can't do what you love and pay the rent. And I'd like to invite you to suspend your disbelief for a moment, because what if it were possible? There are people out there doing it, which means it might be possible for you, too. You can slowly introduce more joy and purpose into your life, while also getting your needs met. Remember, one step at a time does it.

There is no magic way of letting go of your conditioning. What has worked for me has been to become aware of my reactions. As I've done that, I've gone from noticing afterward that I reacted to something, to stopping myself before the reaction takes over.

It's a gradual process that begins with awareness. And the more awareness you have in your life, the more choice you have.

The problem is that these automatic reactions can block you from following you heart. Your heart may nudge you to get started on that novel, but then you start thinking about all the ways things could go wrong, and so you do nothing.

You don't have to change your personality. All you have to do is start noticing these internal reactions, because simply shining a light in the darkness will start the process of change.

When you begin to notice how your reactions are creating either joy or suffering in your life, you immediately have more choice. You don't have to try and change anything. Simply notice how you react in different situations.

Heart-Based Action Steps

Today, notice how you react to things. It can be tricky at first, because sometimes your reactions can be so automatic that you don't even notice them until they're over. Simply do your best, and let things unfold naturally.

To get you started, here are your action steps for today:

1. **Become aware of your reactions.** The process for learning how you experience reality is quite simple. It starts with becoming aware of your reactions. When you notice your internal patterns, you can decide whether they're useful or not. Don't expect them to go away, but simply let them be there. Many people live without awareness of how they react to life. They believe it's just the way things are, which immediately stops them from changing and tapping into more joy.

2. **Focus on everyday matters.** Don't go after the heavy stuff right away. Instead, look at how you react when you drop something on the floor, when you stub your toe, or when you're standing in line at the store. Observe what's going on, and pay particular attention to what happens inside of you.

3. **It's a gradual process.** Many of your reactions have been with you for years, so changing them may take time. If you find yourself getting frustrated, you're pushing too hard. Take a step back, relax, and let it happen at the pace it happens. There's no rush.

Day 3: Do Your Best

If you want to live a happy life, you have to accept the fact that you can only do your best. One way to do so is to stop pushing so hard. When you run into frustration, it's a sign that you need to take a step back, because you're trying to do something you cannot do.

Most people are their own worst enemy. Nothing they do is good enough. When they succeed, they find fault in themselves. When they fail, they plunge into misery. I know, because I've been there.

Just a few short years ago, I used to work until I was exhausted. I had a goal, and I wanted to get to the end as soon as possible. Nothing was good enough until I'd reached my goal. Eventually, I realized that even when I achieved each goal, I wasn't any happier. I just set a new goal, and the cycle would start all over again.

As I've gotten more experience with trusting my heart, I've realized that I can only do the best with what I have. While this may sound simplistic, you may be surprised at how often you try to push yourself.

Somehow we've learned that we have to constantly give 110% of ourselves in everything we do. This means we have to work more, do more, and accomplish more, even if we're already operating at maximum capacity.

When I'm working on my business, I know I'm pushing myself too hard when I run into frustration, fear, and overwhelm. Your feelings will tell you if you're on the right track or not. If I'm stuck and try to force progress, I'll encounter frustration. It's a reminder for me to focus on doing what I can. Not more, not less.

The key is to take a break. What's important to note is that it is when I least want to take a break that I need to take one the most. When I'm frustrated and angry about not making progress, I want to prove to myself that I can do it anyway, but that's when I know I have to step back. I might go and watch a movie, hang out with my son, or go for a walk. I'll do anything but work.

When I work with people who want to build an online business around something they enjoy, I notice that they want to succeed so badly that they push themselves over the edge. They forget that things take time and that there are no shortcuts. You have to put in the work, and you have to let your brain assimilate what you're learning.

Doing your best isn't about avoiding frustration, but about knowing where and when to stop. It's about pushing yourself to the edge but not over the edge. And it's about realizing that you can trust your heart to lead the way. You don't have to follow society's rules of constantly doing more, because that's a sure-fire path to unhappiness.

Instead, you can relax, knowing that you're doing your best. Even when you fail to listen to your heart, you're still trying, and as long as you improve and try again, all is well. When you do your best, you not only feel good, but your life flows more easily.

Heart-Based Action Steps

Doing your best comes down to taking your foot off the gas. It's about realizing that instead of operating at 100%, you can go at 80%.

Follow Your Heart

To help you get started on doing your best, try these tips:

1. **Stop the madness.** Start by taking a close look at how you push yourself. What do you tell yourself that makes you think that you aren't already good enough? What makes you think that doing your best isn't enough? Where does it come from?

2. **Just for today.** Experiment with doing your best. If you're a Type-A personality like I am, try operating at 70% of your maximum capacity. Have a more relaxed pace today. Notice when you're being hard on yourself, and back off. Tell your mind that you're trying this out just for today.

3. **Take breaks.** The last thing you probably want to do is to take breaks, but breaks help your brain and heart consolidate what you're doing and learning. It'll keep you sharp, and it'll help you gain more clarity about whatever challenges you're facing. Keep your breaks simple and enjoyable, but take real breaks. Even ten minutes can make a big difference.

Day 4: Open Your Heart

Just a few years ago, I was cynical and unhappy. Everything I did had to make logical sense. I didn't even know you could live life through your heart. Don't get me wrong, logic still has its place. This isn't about mind versus heart, but learning to incorporate both.

Today, my life is different, and my mind is a servant to my heart. I now realize that deep down, we're all the same. We have the same fears and desires. We are all made of stardust.

When you walk past a beggar, remember that he wants the same core things you do. He wants to be happy and to avoid pain. When you give your money to the clerk at your supermarket, remember that she has her own challenges in life. She worries about money, and she worries about how life will turn out, just like you do.

When you connect to other people like this, it opens your heart. When you realize that you are not alone with what you're going through, it immediately lifts the heavy brick off of your chest. You realize that what you're experiencing is normal.

We're so used to closing our heart and building a protective wall around it. This separates you from everyone else. It creates loneliness and makes matters worse. I'm not saying you have to blindly trust anyone, but you can still open your heart.

Just a few days ago, I went to the mall to buy some groceries (my supermarket is in the mall). As I walked past people, I noticed that the vast majority of them had stern faces. Their hearts were full of worry and fear. At that moment I was reminded that beneath those faces—no matter how unfriendly they appeared—were vulnerable hearts, and unfulfilled desires.

It doesn't matter what we look like, what color our skin is, or where we're from, because in the end, we're all part of the human family. Immediately when I brought this to mind, my heart opened. I'm sure people looked at me and wondered why I was smiling.

So to open my heart, I focused on the fact that we're all connected. We all have the same fears and dreams. I want my life to turn out well, and so does everyone else.

This is not about pitying anyone, which separates you from everyone else. Instead, it's about compassion, and knowing that even with all the suffering in the world, we can do our best, and we can hold that suffering in the warm embrace of our hearts.

Buddhists have a meditation called lovingkindness, where they focus on other people, and send them loving thoughts. I sometimes use it when I'm out and about. As I walk past people, I bring my attention to my heart and silently repeat, "May you be healthy. May you be happy. May you be free from suffering." The words don't matter as much as the wishing other people well. If you have resistance to wishing other people well, start by doing this on yourself. Simply replace the you with I.

Just a few years ago, this all seemed like mumbo jumbo to me, but the more I've opened up, the better I've started to feel. The bottom line is that we're all in this together, and we're all doing our best.

Heart-Based Action Steps

Today you're going to practice opening your heart. Gradually, as you peel off the layers around your heart, you'll start to tap into joy and peace, and it'll help you connect to the true desires of your heart.
Here are your three action steps for today:

1. **Focus on your heart.** To open your heart, start by connecting to it, just as we did in the first chapter. Bring attention to your heart, and feel what's going on. In the early stages of opening your heart, you may experience grief or suffering that's been there for a long time. You don't have to try and get rid of it. Just feel it.

2. **Wish yourself well.** The first step is to wish yourself well. Simply say, "May I be healthy. May I be happy. May I be free from suffering." Repeat this over and over for as long as you feel comfortable. Also, remember that you do not have to feel anything specific. When you first begin this practice, you probably won't feel your heart opening right away. Just keep doing it, and see what happens.

3. **Wish other people well.** When you're out and about today, look at the people you meet and remember that they too have their own problems and challenges in life. Silently wish them well. Wish for them to be happy, healthy, and free from suffering. If envy, judgment, or other thoughts come up, let them be, and keep opening your heart. If you want more on this topic, I recommend the

Follow Your Heart

book, *Lovingkindness: The Revolutionary Art of Happiness*, by Sharon Salzberg.

Day 5: Befriend Fear

When it comes to living a heart-based life, fear can stop you dead in your tracks. You don't have to get rid of fear, but you can't run away from it. If you let your fears dictate how you live, you'll end up with an unfulfilling life.

As you start trusting your heart more, you'll notice that there's often a war going on between your mind and your heart. Your heart may nudge you in one direction, and things may go well at first, but then your internal thermostat kicks in.

A thermostat is made to regulate temperature and to keep it within a certain range. Your mind will try to do the same thing. It wants to keep you in your comfort zone. It wants to keep you safe.

Following your heart means doing something new. It means changing the way you do things. This is why I recommend you take tiny steps, because if you try to make radical changes, your thermostat may kick in.

I'm reminded of a time when I was just starting out doing work I love. I was shaking in my boots, because I didn't know what I was doing, but my heart kept nudging me to take one step at a time.

As I kept moving forward, I discovered that the key to befriending fear is not to try and eliminate it, but to let it be there, and to keep putting one foot in front of the other. It wasn't comfortable, but with each step, my fears fell away. I also noticed that as one fear fell away, it was replaced by another.

This is how life is. We're here to grow, and in order to grow, we need challenges. This means that fear may always be a part of your life, so getting rid of fears isn't the goal. The goal is to learn to relate to your fears in a new way.

For example, when my son, Vincent, was born, I was afraid. I worried about whether or not I would be a good father. But I also knew that I could only do my best, so I didn't take my fears too seriously. I let them be there, and I opened up my heart to them. It is this space that I'm pointing to when I talk about relating to fear in a new way. You don't have to believe in every thought you have. If you can stay with your fears, and feel them fully, a new world will open up.

Most people get completely entangled in their fears and worries. It's easy to forget that you are the director. You can take a deep breath and let your fears be, without getting involved. It's definitely not easy, and it doesn't happen overnight, but it does work.

You don't have to run away from fear. Instead, face fear like a warrior. Every fear you have is an opportunity to train. It's an opportunity to strengthen the connection you have with your heart and your intuition.

The more you challenge your fears, the less power they will have over you. You've probably heard the advice of facing your fears, and while it is obvious, it doesn't make it any less effective. Sometimes the smartest thing you can do is to dive into the suffering inside of you, because that is the only way you can discover what's underneath it all.

Fear can keep you from joy, or it can be the door to it. It's a door with a lot of special effects, but once you walk through it, you'll see that it was all for show. Just like movies can feel real, so can fear falsely intimidate you into dismissing the nudges of your heart.

Heart-Based Action Steps

Today, make a game out of befriending fear. We're used to taking our fears and thoughts so seriously that we lose ourselves in them. It may feel like there is no other way, but that's because you're so used to doing things this way.

Here are your action steps:

1. **Put on your detective hat.** The absolute first step is to notice the tiny fears that dictate your life. Do you go to a certain store because you're afraid of something in another? Start noticing these fears, and challenge them.

2. **Welcome your fears.** Once you notice fear, breathe it into your heart. I like to think of this as opening the door to an old friend, and welcoming him or her in. Pushing fear away doesn't work, so I simply stop, and breathe.

3. **Make it a game.** The more fun you have doing this, the easier it'll be. Start by challenging tiny fears and the mindset will naturally ripple to the rest of your life. But let it happen at its own pace. Have fun and remember that fear is here to challenge you to grow. Face it like the warrior you are.

Day 6: Be Yourself

Sally Hogshead, author of *Fascinate*, said, "You don't have to change who you are to become your most successful. In fact, it's the opposite. You need to become more of who you are."

Being yourself isn't about trying to be some version of yourself that you aren't already. It's about stripping away the layers of shoulds. It means being comfortable in your own skin, whether you think you fit into society or not, because in the end, you can only be who you are. Trying to be someone else is a waste of energy.

We spend an immense amount of energy trying to fit into the image other people create for us. We naturally want the approval of our peers, but how far are we willing to go? Some live their whole life according to what other people think is right. They neglect their heart, and then they wonder why they feel so empty and unfulfilled. They live lives of silent desperation, because they've lost themselves in a sea of conformity.

Being yourself means being okay with your own desires. It means trusting the guidance you get from your heart. If you want to start playing guitar, start without thinking about what other people may think.

When you don't feel like you can trust your own heart, you start looking to other people for advice. You give your power away, and you believe someone else can help you live a life that will make you happy. You've been told your whole life what you should do, and it doesn't work. You have to take responsibility. And you have to let go of the layers of shoulds and start listening to your true desires.

The truth of the matter is that you are good enough. You don't have to put on a mask. You don't have to be someone else. Many of our problems come from believing that we are not good enough as we are. But you can only be who you are right now, and the sooner you can accept that, the happier you'll be.

Try it out right now. Take a deep breath, and just for a few seconds, feel what it's like to fully accept yourself, with quirks and all. You don't have to be "perfect," because perfect is a label someone else has created. That label contains characteristics of what perfect should be, and most likely, you can never live up to it, and even if you could, it wouldn't make you happy, because you wouldn't be true to your heart.

In the end, what will make you happy and fulfilled is listening to your heart. It's as simple, and as hard, as that. It's a process that begins by noticing the shoulds in your life, and letting them go.

Heart-Based Action Steps

Being who you are is not about adding more to yourself, but about stripping away what doesn't belong.

Here are your three action steps for today:

1. **Find the conflict.** Where do you have shoulds stopping you from expressing your heart? What do you want to do that you aren't doing because of what other people might think? What do you feel like you have to lie about in order to fit in? Notice where these conflicts are. There's nothing you have

to do but be aware of how you're holding yourself back.

2. **Uncover the pull.** Next, look at what those shoulds are preventing you from doing. What do you secretly want to do? What does your heart desire? Notice the conflict and let it go. Letting go simply means being willing to take the first step despite the discomfort.

3. **Let it happen.** This is a gradual process that happens over time, at least it was for me. There's no need to rush things. Instead, do what you can with what you have. Think small, instead of big. And remember that it all starts with awareness.

Day 7: Stop Waiting

My son doesn't like to color within the lines. He doesn't even like to color on paper. He draws on tables, floors, walls, and even tries to draw on our dog. He hasn't yet learned what's right or wrong. You can try to tell him, but chances are that he won't understand. At least not yet.

Children unabashedly follow their inner urge to experiment, learn, and play. Somewhere along the line you learn what's right and wrong. You learn to color within the lines, because that's how things should be done.

In order to live the life of your dreams, you have to stop looking for permission from anyone. You have to be willing to draw outside the lines and see what happens.

Your friends, family, and society in general won't understand what it means to live a heart-based life. It doesn't make sense to them.

Don't try to change their mind, because it will only make them dig their heels deeper. Instead, let them be, and keep following your joy, inspiration, and passion.

A few years ago, I had a brief stint with Aikido, a Japanese martial art. When I first entered the dojo, I was hesitant, and I constantly looked for permission from the teacher. Each technique we learned, I wondered if I was doing it right. As the months passed, I kept doing my thing. I kept hesitating, apologizing, and wondering if I was doing things correctly. But one day, I experienced a shift. I realized that the only way I was going to become better was if I made the teachings and techniques my own.

I realized that I had to stop looking for permission and own my actions. I had to stop waiting until I was a black belt, and I had to use what I had right now.

Once this shift happened, my improvement was obvious. I even got a compliment from the teacher, which is rare here in Finland, where even a nod of the head is considered high praise.

This realization not only affected my Aikido, but the rest of my life as well. I stopped waiting, and I began moving toward what I wanted, without apologizing, and without looking for permission. I realized that no one could tell me what was right for me.

This didn't mean I was now unstoppable. It simply meant that I was willing to stop looking outside of myself for answers.

Many of the people I talk to know what their hearts want, but they are held back. They are waiting for something. It could be money, approval, talent, or opportunity. The truth is that you have to be willing to start with what you have.

When I started my online business, I started from scratch. I made excuses for a long time about why I couldn't start until one day I had had enough. I started listening to my inspiration, and I started doing what made my heart sing.

I'm not going to lie. It's uncomfortable to go against the grain, but if you want to be happy and fulfilled, you have to stop looking for answers outside of yourself. It is by following your truth, and your joy, that you'll find lasting happiness.

Heart-Based Action Steps

You've probably noticed that I keep nudging you to listen to your heart, and to let go of anything that stops you. The reason is simple: the more you even imagine listening to your heart, the more the joy in your life will expand.

Here are your action steps for today:

1. **Identify.** Identify what you're waiting for. You know the life you want to live, so what's stopping you? If you don't know what you want, what's stopping you from listening to your heart and taking the next step? Look at the reasons why you aren't taking the next step.

2. **See through.** Your excuses will seem as immovable as Mt. Everest, but they aren't. Everest isn't conquered in one leap, but by taking one step at a time. And it is by taking one step at a time that you'll uncover the joy and purpose already present in your life. You may have a light bulb moment like I did, or you may not. Whatever happens will be right for you.

3. **Start where you are.** Many of the reasons why we wait are because we believe we don't have what we need to get started. The truth is that you always have what you need. You have to be willing to start with what you have, where you are, and let things evolve from there. Look at how you can start, and then start.

Day 8: Get on the Right Track

If you're like most people, you worry whether or not you're on the right track. You worry about if your life is turning out okay. You want your life to be the best it can be, so you constantly think about whether or not you're making the right decisions.

But what if it was enough to simply follow your heart and trust that you were where you needed to be? We judge our progress by how good our life is going, but we forget that sometimes life will look bad before it gets better.

You have no idea what's around the corner. You don't know that in order to get your dream job, you may first have to lose your current job. We believe we know what one event in our life means, but we don't.

This is why the best way to be on track in your life is not to try to obsessively figure everything out, but to listen to your inner GPS. It also means not berating yourself for not following your heart 100% of the time. It means trusting that life is unfolding in the way it should, even if you make the "wrong" decisions.

Your heart doesn't give you a step-by-step list of what you need to do to get what you want. Instead, it guides you toward what you need.

Your heart is flexible. When the world around you changes, your heart knows where you need to go. But if you make rigid plans and things change, like they always do, you end up confused.

One day I was walking to the gym, and there was a heavy fog in the air. I couldn't see more than a few feet

Follow Your Heart

in front of me. As I was walking, I realized that in order to see more, I had to keep walking. This seems obvious when you're walking in a fog, but somehow we forget about it when living life.

When you follow your heart, you often won't know where you're going. You may have a destination in mind, but there's fog all around you. You feel confused, overwhelmed, and lost, because you're trying to figure things out. You stop moving forward, and you stand still, trying to figure out the best path, when the best path is simply to take one step at a time.

In my life, I've noticed that the more willing I am to let go of trying to figure out the future, the happier I am. I can't control what's coming, but what I can do is connect to my inner GPS, my heart, which guides me in the right direction through the feelings I have.

One of the biggest obstacles you'll run into when following your heart is that at times things won't make sense logically. You'll feel lost, and disaster scenarios will swirl out of control in your mind. That's normal. It's your mind's attempt to keep you safe.

But what will determine whether or not you "succeed" is how steadfast you are when the going gets rough.

So in the end, there is no right track, because there are many paths that lead to a fulfilling life. One of the best paths I've found is to listen to my heart. It's not an easy path, but it will gradually help you turn up the happiness in your life.

Heart-Based Action Steps

Knowing whether or not you're on the right track isn't as important as follow your inspiration. Go toward what makes your heart sing, and what brings joy to your life. Here's how you can play with this today:

1. **Take a heart-based step.** Instead of thinking about what you're going to do with your life, or how you're going to find your purpose, bring your attention to your heart, and play with taking a heart-based step. Notice where your heart wants to go, and go there. It could just mean sitting down and doing some journaling. It could be anything. Don't worry about doing things right or wrong. Don't worry about where things may lead. Instead, experiment with walking in the fog and trusting your heart.

2. **Embrace the mystery.** Realize that you can never figure life out. No one has a crystal ball. At least no one I know of. So why frustrate yourself? You'll only drain your own energy. Instead, relax, and just for today, let go of figuring anything out. Let life come to you, and stay in the present moment.

3. **Confusion is not a problem.** Eckhart Tolle once said 'Confusion is not I don't know. It's I don't know, but I should know.' And the truth of the matter is that you don't need to know everything about life. Your heart will know and it will guide you one step at a time. I'm repeating myself, but I want to drill this point home.

Day 9: Simplify

The more I simplify my life, the better I feel. There's something about holding onto stuff that weighs you down.

This isn't about living with 40 items, but about living with the essentials. What those essentials are will differ from person to person. If you have a family and a house, you'll need more than a single guy in his 20's.

But the core benefit remains the same. When you let go of the stuff you don't need, you feel lighter. It creates a vacuum in your life for other things to enter.

If you've accumulated a lot of stuff you don't need, it's a symptom of a deeper problem. There's an anxiety behind all that needing to buy that you haven't addressed. Once you're willing to feel it, you'll decrease the amount of unnecessary buying that you do, and you'll start giving things away.

You could give away one piece of clothing, a book, or eliminate sugar from your diet for a week. Think tiny, doable steps. And if small steps aren't enough, try mini steps. For example, if you can't eliminate sugar for a whole week, start by eliminating it for one hour, and gradually increase it to two hours, three hours, and so on.

As you simplify your life, you'll notice that there's a sense of spaciousness that opens up inside of you. Your heart begins to feel lighter. It's not just the giving aspect that feels good, but your heart relaxes. It's almost as if clinging to things depletes your energy.

You can take this too far though. I'm naturally frugal, which means I'll put off buying things if I can,

Follow Your Heart

but it goes too far when I delay buying something that I need, such as new equipment for my business.

Simplifying your life doesn't have to be complex, nor does it have to be overwhelming. You can start by giving away something small, such as a book or a piece of clothing. Just get started and notice how good it feels to give.

It's easy to fall into the trap of thinking that the more stuff we have, the happier we'll be. But I think you've been around for long enough to know that it isn't true. All you end up with is stuff you don't need.

Material possessions can never bring you happiness, because happiness comes from the inside, and happiness comes from, you guessed it, following your heart. The hole you feel can never be filled with things, or food, or alcohol, or sex. It can only be filled by drinking the vitamins and minerals from your heart.

In short, simplifying your life is about removing what you no longer need. Each person is different, and your needs will be different from mine. That is why cookie cutter advice rarely works. Listen to your heart, and uncover what is best for you, because once you do, you'll feel happier and lighter.

Heart-Based Action Steps

Remember, you don't have to start big. You don't have to move to a tiny apartment. You don't have to give away your whole wardrobe. Just start small.

Here are your action steps for the day:

1. **Start small.** Find something that's been gathering dust for months, or even years, and give it away, or

sell it. It could be a book, old clothes, or even an old computer. Whatever you do, start by getting rid of something easy.

2. **Keep going.** After you've given away something small, give away something else. You don't have to do it right away, but make it a habit to simplify your life. Notice how good it feels to get rid of something, and give it to someone who actually needs it.

3. **Wait.** When you get an impulse to buy something, instead of buying it right away, wait. If you want a new phone, computer, or whatever it is, wait for 30 days before you buy. Look at your buying patterns. When do you tend to buy things? Is it when you feel anxious, or when you feel stressed out from work? Could you avoid buying something just once? Experiment with this, and keep it light.

Day 10: Make Right Decisions

We want to make the right decisions. The problem is that we try to make decisions based on the information we have, and that information is often incomplete, because you don't know all the variables in play. And you certainly don't know what the future will bring, but still you do what you can and hope for the best.

You can't rely on your mind alone to make decisions. It may feel comforting to make decisions that make sense logically, but logic doesn't guarantee happiness.

This doesn't mean you should blindly follow your impulses and wreck your whole life. Following your heart is deeper than your impulses.

Remember in the first chapter when I shared how I used my heart to buy a house? I wasn't in a rush to make a decision, because I knew that in order to get a clear signal from my heart, I had to let my mind settle down, and I did that by waiting and giving things time.

When I make a decision, I wait. I used to rush decisions, and I've done it enough times to know that it doesn't lead to anything good. This doesn't mean you have to wait days to make every decision in your life. You should still use common sense. Some decisions require time, while others don't.

What I avoid, if possible, is making decisions when I'm in a negative state of mind. It's tricky, because when you feel bad, there's a sense of urgency to act. On some level, we believe that making a decision will get rid of the negative feeling, but it won't.

The best thing you can do when you feel bad is to let the storm pass, and come to a decision when you feel better. What should you do in the meantime? Do whatever you want. Watch a movie, take a walk, read a book, or spend time with the people you love.

This won't always be practical. There are times when you need to make a decision right away. When that happens, do your best to calm down before you decide. Give yourself a chance to connect to your heart.

For example, when I made the decision to buy our house, I first got an initial feeling, which was good. But I still wasn't sure, so I waited, and with a few nights' sleep, things became clearer.

Our brains are hardwired against being patient. Why do you think TV series utilize cliffhangers? It's because we go crazy when something is left unanswered or unsolved. The same is true for problems in your life. You'll want to solve them right away, but you'll make the best decisions when you give your heart time to make its voice heard.

Remember, you don't have to rush decisions, even though you may feel a sense of urgency. Avoid making any decision when you're in a negative state of mind. It won't always be possible, but do your best.

Heart-Based Action Steps

Making decisions is a lot of fun when you let go of taking everything so seriously. You can take the stress out of decisions by including your heart in the decision making process, and by waiting for a few days before you act.

Here are three tips on how you can do that:

Follow Your Heart

1. **Wait.** Just like with buying things, the longer you can wait, the clearer the decision will become. If you're in a hurry to decide, you're prone to make mistakes. Forget about the urgency that most problems come with. They are not urgent just because they feel urgent. Wait until you feel better and have a better connection to your heart.

2. **Be still.** Meditate, run, walk, play music, draw, knit, or do whatever helps you get into a peaceful, meditative state of mind. That's where your heart will have a clear communication channel to you. This is why we often get insights in the shower, while washing dishes, or working out.

3. **Notice.** Once the storm has passed, notice which decision feels magnetic? What pulls you toward it? You may have fear, or you may not. But your heart will be drawn to a particular decision. You do not have to solve every problem in your life right away. You don't have to rush decisions. Let them be and let your heart come up with an inspired answer when the time is right.

Day 11: Unleash Your Inner Artist

We all have an artist inside of us. You might've been told that you're not talented or artistic, but that's hogwash. This isn't about being the next Leonardo Da Vinci, but about expressing what's in your heart.

Deep down, you have an urge to express yourself. When you were younger, you enjoyed the artistic side of you. At some point, it was drummed out of you. You stopped believing in yourself.

Unleashing your inner artist means listening to your heart, and starting. It's another way to be yourself, and do your best, because until you embrace the whole you, and all your heart's nudges, you won't feel complete.

For a long time, I didn't think I could draw. I still remember when I was six or seven. I sat at my desk in my room, trying to draw, but it wasn't as good as the artists I was comparing myself against. Eventually, I got so frustrated that I threw the paper and pens on the floor, and I thought to myself, "I'll never be good at this, so I might as well give up. I hate drawing."

It took me twenty years before I decided to challenge that statement. In June 2012, I joined a cartooning course, and I've been drawing daily ever since. I started off barely being able to draw a stick figure. Today, I can draw landscapes, and funny cartoons, all because I was willing to start. I realized that just because I thought I wasn't an artist didn't mean it was true.

I faced many inner demons along the way. I wanted to quit because I didn't feel good enough, and I compared myself to others. Despite all this, I kept putting one foot in front of the other.

Unleashing your inner artist starts by noticing what you've secretly wanted to do all these years. It could be painting, sculpting, playing guitar, writing, or something else. There is always some unexpressed desire.

The biggest mistake you can make is to think you have to be fantastic at what you do according to someone else's standard. If you pick up the guitar today, you won't be great. You won't be able to produce good sounding chords, because you first have to learn how to hold the guitar, how to hold your fingers, and how to strum. So take the stress out of performing, and allow yourself to play.

Don't worry about picking the right thing. Just start somewhere, and even if you pick up the guitar today, and stop three months later, it's fine. This is about exploration, not about getting a result.

When you follow your heart, you'll notice that you get creative urges. It doesn't just have to be in art, so don't limit yourself. Explore freely, experiment, and above all, have fun.

Heart-Based Action Steps

Whatever your heart is telling you, listen to it. Notice how your heart wants to express itself artistically.

In order to unleash your inner artist, you have to open your heart, and you have to open yourself up to life. Here are three tips on how you can get started:

Follow Your Heart

1. **Forget about results.** You don't have to be talented to do something. I'm learning to draw one day at a time. In our society, some things are associated with talent. But talented people are often overshadowed by people who are consistent and put in the work. Whatever you want to do, begin it. Forget about where it may lead.

2. **Find your inner artist.** Identify what it is that you've always wanted to do. Your mind may rebel, but your heart will say yes. Focus on taking the next step, and don't put pressure on yourself to make anything out of it. If there are no classes or courses near you, find some tutorials online, and get started.

3. **The magic of daily practice.** The way to get better at anything is to practice daily. If you want to write a book, start writing daily, even if it is for just 15 minutes. If you want to learn to play the guitar, start picking away every day. It takes time to get good. When frustration comes up, center yourself in the present moment, and find a way to enjoy what you do.

Day 12: Flow with Life

Being in flow with life means seeing life as it truly is—full of uncertainty and change. We tend to cling to how things are. We resist the very nature of life, and when life changes, we suffer.

When you realize that life is constantly coming and going, you relax, and you realize that it's okay to surrender and go with the flow.

If you resist life, your life will be full of pain and stress. You'll constantly try to manipulate life in order to get what you want. If you succeed, your perfect life will eventually change, and you will suffer. So you see, whichever way you look at it, you'll suffer if you are too attached to how things are. It's much easier to turn your boat downstream and go with the flow.

For example, the work I do right now revolves around creating my own programs and books, but there was a time when I worked with freelance clients. However, I found that whenever I would do freelance work, I'd resist it, and I always had trouble getting clients. After awhile, it became obvious that I was trying to swim upstream. I didn't truly enjoy the work. It was fun, but it didn't set my heart on fire. Once I stopped trying to get more freelance clients, I started looking at what I truly enjoyed doing.

The way to flow with life is to realize that you have a GPS inside of you. Your heart is like the GPS in a car. It will tell you where to go next, but you have to be willing to listen to it.

You can still make plans, but be prepared to change them. Stay flexible, because your heart doesn't care about your plans. It cares about what's right for you, and what you are meant to do.

This has been obvious in my life. I've made plans, but each time I've thought I knew where I was going, I've been proven wrong. I now have a direction of where I'm going, and I listen to my heart, but I try not to make any rigid plans.

I don't have a goal of becoming rich, famous, or successful. I simply want to express what's in my heart, because I know that that is what will ultimately expand the happiness and joy in my life.

Tapping into the flow of life won't get rid of challenges in your life. Life is full of problems, because that's how life works. Life wouldn't be interesting if you didn't have a few obstacles, would it?

What will make a difference is how you relate to life. You'll no longer expect life to remain the same. You'll no longer believe that you have complete control over what goes on.

Life is change. The only certainty is uncertainty. The sooner you embrace that, the happier you'll be. To tap into the flow, look at where your heart is pulling you. Look at what you're excited about, and look at where the stream of life is trying to take you.

Heart-Based Action Steps

To flow with life, make loose plans and be open to new ideas and to your heart pulling you in a new direction.

Here's how you can experiment with introducing more flow into your life today:

1. **Identify resistance.** Where in your life do you resist change? Where are you trying to swim upstream? You'll often have a logical reason for doing this, but imagine for a moment that you let go. What would it look like to turn your boat downstream?

2. **Experiment with changing your life.** Start small. Take a new road to work. Read a new book. Do something that scares you a bit. Listen to your heart, and take bold steps forward. As you do this, you'll notice that change isn't so bad. Change is a part of life, and trying to resist it will only make you suffer. Ultimately, it is not change that causes suffering, but your resistance to it.

3. **Be flexible.** Just for today, be flexible in your thinking. Be ready to change whatever plans you have, and be ready to follow your heart. You don't have to make rigid plans and stick to schedules to live a happy life. In fact, they can often keep you from living a life full of purpose and happiness. Keep the plans you need for practical purposes, but just for today, open up and plug into your heart.

Day 13: Be Still

If you truly want to live a heart-based life, there's no better way than to learn to be still, or to meditate for a few minutes every single day.

Meditation does not mean sitting cross-legged for hours on end. You can meditate right now while you're reading this. Simply become aware of your breathing as you read. That's all. Just notice your breath going in and out.

Meditation has changed my life. I started meditating daily in 2005. I've had breaks here and there, but mostly I've stuck to it, and the changes in my life have been tremendous. I've gone from feeling lost, angry, and unfulfilled, to being happy, fulfilled, and better able to deal with the stresses of life. I'm not perfect, but the change is like night and day. And most importantly, meditation has helped me gain deeper access to my inner wisdom.

Meditation calms your mind, relaxes your body, and helps you connect to your heart. It won't feel like it when you start, because your mind will be speeding along, because that's what it's used to doing. Simply being aware of the fact that your mind is racing is enough.

You don't have to quiet your mind. In fact, you don't have to do anything, except notice what's going on. If you think of your mind as a TV screen, all you have to do is observe what goes on. When you get pulled into the drama of your thoughts, bring yourself back to observation mode.

There are many ways to meditate. You could count your breath, notice your breath, notice your body, or be mindful of your thoughts. I personally enjoy bringing attention to my body and my feelings, because I spend enough time in my mind as it is.

Don't worry if you're doing things right. All you "should" do is sit and be. You don't have to quiet your mind. You don't have to count your breaths properly, or visualize anything. All you have to do is be aware of what is going on.

In this book, my goal is not to give you superficial strategies, but strategies that have made a difference in my life, and meditation is one of those strategies.

To get started, sit for one minute per day, and notice your breath. If you want, you can count your breaths. So count one when you breathe in, and count two when you breathe out. When you get to ten, start over.

If you're too busy to even spend a minute meditating, you can meditate while you're doing other tasks. If you're washing dishes, notice the water running over your hands and your breath going in and out.

If you're buying groceries, notice what thoughts run through your mind, and become aware of your body as you walk through the aisles.

The only mistake you can make is to not meditate. You can't do this wrong, so just get started, do it in whatever way makes sense to you. You can always course correct later, but don't put this off, because it will change your life.

Heart-Based Action Steps

Meditation can be a hard habit to cultivate, because there are rarely immediate rewards. Nonetheless, it is well worth it, and it will help you turn up the happiness in your life.

Here are three small tips on how you can get started:

1. **Focus on your breath.** Start by being still for one minute per day. Sit down, and focus on your breath going in and out. Don't worry about quieting your mind or staying focused. When your mind wanders, which it will, bring it back to your breath. When your minute is up, stop. After a week, increase the time to two minutes, or whatever you feel comfortable with.

2. **Find your meditation.** Most people have an aversion to sitting still with themselves. It's too painful. Be aware of this aversion, and do your best. You can also use other ways to meditate, such as running, walking, gardening, or whatever you enjoy doing. This is called active meditation. Be aware of your breath, or your body, while you're doing what you're doing.

3. **Stick with it.** The secret to success is to be consistent. It's better to meditate one minute per day for a year rather than 365 minutes once per year. If you don't have time, you can still meditate for one minute. You can be aware of your breath while you walk or commute to work.

Day 14: Let Your Heart Drive

Letting your heart drive means letting go of control. It's about discovering what it feels like to stop manipulating your life.

At first you may feel apprehensive, because you're used to controlling, but as you play with this, you'll uncover a sense of lightness in letting your life unfold naturally. This is because we spend so much time and energy trying to figure out where to go, what to do, and how to make our life turn out exactly the way we want.

For a long time, I thought I could control life. I tried to figure everything out. I wanted guarantees before I embarked on any path. I suffered when things didn't go my way. Eventually, I reached a breaking point, and I realized I had nothing to lose by letting go. So I let go, and the sense of joy was immense. I still go back and forth between control and letting go, because I'm human, and because we never stop growing.

I know I'm trying to control when I get frustrated, angry, and overwhelmed. These are all signs that I'm trying to do something I can't do. Often when one of these signs pops up, I'll go sit on the couch, close my eyes, and breathe for a moment.

Let me give you an example of how I let my heart drive. If I feel stressed, I'll sit down, and focus on my breathing for a few minutes to calm down. Then I'll bring my attention to the center of my chest and notice what it wants to tell me.

From there, it comes down to what this book is all about: listening to my heart and noticing where I feel

Follow Your Heart

nudged to go. If I don't feel nudged to go anywhere, I'll look at where I'm trying to control life. This will immediately show me where I can let my heart help me. If I still don't feel anything, I'll look at what interests me, and what I would like to do.

As you start giving up control, you'll have thoughts trying to stop you. They'll tell you that you can't live life this way. They'll tell you that it is irresponsible. But what they leave out is that it's irresponsible to not follow your heart. Responsibility doesn't mean anything if you're making yourself (and the people around you) miserable. And in the end, this isn't about neglecting your responsibilities. It's about taking on more responsibility by finally listening to your heart.

You'll still make plans and live life the way you're used to living it. The difference is that you now have access to another advisor. You still live life like anyone else, but you're also connected to something deeper.

When you stop trying to control and manipulate life, you'll start to feel lighter and happier. And remember, don't try to overhaul your whole life. Instead play with this, and let things happen at their natural pace.

In summary, letting my heart drive means noticing where I'm trying to control things, and then taking a step back. It doesn't mean neglecting my life. It means that I see that I'm not in complete control, and that I can ask for help from my heart.

Heart-Based Action Steps

Today, experiment with letting your heart drive. To make it palatable for your mind, tell your mind that you're going to conduct a little experiment.

Here are three tips for letting go:

1. **Imagine being the passenger.** Imagine for a moment that you were never in control of your life. This may feel uncomfortable, but try it on and play with it. You can always go back to your old ways later. Let go of the steering wheel and hand over control to your heart. Let it guide you, just for today.

2. **Learn how your heart works.** In order to get help from your heart, you have to learn how your heart works. I can't tell you what to do, because you have to discover how your heart communicates with you. My heart communicates mostly via feeling, like I mentioned in the beginning of this book. I feel inspired to do something, or I don't.

3. **The truth.** Realize that you were never in total control in the first place. Look at some of the most significant events in your life. Look at all the different variables that had to be in place for them to happen. It's a wonderful cosmic soup. Experiment with this and uncover what works for you. If something doesn't feel right for you, mold it to your liking.

Day 15: Play

You can't connect to your heart if you're taking this too seriously. There is no one testing you. You don't have to live up to anyone's expectations. All you have to do is play with life.

When you start living from your heart, you start taking everything less seriously, because on some level, you see the truth. You see that everything outside of you is in transition. Your body is healthy one moment and sick the next. Your friends come and go. Money comes and goes. Success comes and goes.

Why cling to anything when life is constantly changing? The key is to rediscover the lightness you had as a child, when everything was play and experimentation.

If you examine your life closely, you may notice that you get the best results when you don't take life so seriously. What you want in the end is to be able to play anyway, so why not start right this moment?

Avoid becoming serious about playing. Don't make it another should in your life. Instead, become aware of it after finishing this chapter and let it enter your life naturally, without you trying to control it. In other words, let your inner wisdom determine the right pace.

I became a father in December 2011. My son has been one of my biggest teachers when it comes to enjoying life. He has this tremendous ability to follow his heart. He does what brings him joy. He draws on walls, throws food on the floor, and eats dog food just to see what will happen. He doesn't have goals. He doesn't

Follow Your Heart

even worry about what his purpose is, because he doesn't know what purpose means. Just thinking about him puts me in a more playful mood.

When I find myself getting too serious, what helps me get out of it is to allow myself to be crappy. When I need to introduce more play into my writing, I focus on writing horribly. I stop trying to get a particular result and I just write. When I get too serious about my cartooning, I allow myself to scribble and make a mess.

You might say that it's unrealistic to even compare your life to a child's, but is it really? What's unrealistic is believing that you have to be serious about life. There is no proof that being serious leads to a happier life. In fact, when I look at my life, I see a strong correlation between seriousness and unhappiness.

Being realistic means seeing life for what it truly is—an adventure. Yes, some things in life need focus and determination, but that doesn't mean you have to be serious about it. You can play and still get things done.

"But if I play I'll run out of money and starve to death," you might be thinking. And that is a very common reaction. We've learned that we can't play and get our needs met. I'm not asking you to abandon your life and just play. I'm asking you to see how you can introduce more play into your life. There are people out there doing what they love and paying the bills, so it must be possible, right? It isn't as black and white as you think. You can play with play while paying the bills. Introduce play wherever it makes sense, and let it expand naturally.

Play is your natural state. You can't figure life out. You can't predict the future, so you might as well enjoy what you have right now, and see where life takes you.

Heart-Based Action Steps

Introducing more play into your life doesn't have to be an ordeal. In fact, if you take it too seriously, you'll ruin it. So take a deep breath, relax, and imagine what it would feel like to be more playful.

Here are a few tips on how you can start:

1. **Focus on the present.** Young children are almost constantly in the present moment. They don't worry about the future or regret the past. Older children learn to be serious, which makes them unhappy. In order to play, you have to focus on what's here right now. Let go of trying to control how things will turn out, and enjoy the present moment.

2. **Nothing is serious.** Look at children: they don't take life seriously because they haven't learned that they should. We, on the other hand, take life seriously because there are "serious" things we need to deal with. But do we have to be so serious? No, we don't. Today, notice where you tighten up. What aspects of your life do you think you have to take seriously?

3. **A joyful infusion.** Once you find what makes you serious, experiment with infusing it with play. Ask your heart how you can best do this. I like to center myself in the present moment, and let go of trying to control the end result. It's paradoxical, because once you stop trying so hard, you get better results.

Day 16: Cut Cords

The friends I have today are not the friends I had five years ago. My childhood friends and I slowly drifted apart. It was like one of those magnets you put on your fridge. As they get older, they lose traction and fall to the floor.

As you dive deeper into living a heart-based life, you'll notice that some of your relationships will naturally drift away, and you'll reach a point where you have to cut the cord.

Cutting cords is not as violent as it sounds. When I've drifted apart from friends, it has happened organically. We've just lost touch. We may talk a few times per year when we bump into each other, or via email, but other than that, there's no connection.

When you let old friends and relationships go, it's like letting stuff go from your life. You feel lighter, and you have one less should in your life, because let's face it, if you're spending time with people you'd rather not spend time with, you're draining your own energy.

If you keep spending time with people that don't resonate with you, you'll just end up making yourself unhappy. You may not want to let go, because what if you don't make any new friends? But that's just fear making an appearance, as it always does when change is around the corner.

Your heart will know the right step to take. It may not tell you outright, but it will tell you through the feelings you have.

You don't have to determine upfront who will be your friend, and what kind of relationship you'll be in. You can let things unfold naturally.

Also, something you may find is that after a few years of drifting apart from someone, they may come back into your life, and the connection may be stronger than ever, so you never know where life will take you.

The pitfall I've had to avoid when cutting cords is doing so abruptly. My mind often wants to make it official that I'm no longer friends with someone, but I've found that the best thing I can do is to leave things open. Now, if you're in a romantic relationship, you'd obviously need to tell the other person. So use common sense where appropriate.

While drifting away from friends is never fun, it is what it is. You may once have had a great time with someone, but you've since changed, and it may be time to move on.

Heart-Based Action Steps

You can't keep holding onto a relationship that doesn't resonate with you. It will only drain you of energy and prevent you from following your heart. This isn't popular advice, because we wish it wouldn't come to this, but sometimes you have to say goodbye.

Here are three action steps to help you let go of relationships that are no longer a good fit for you:

1. **Find the stale ones.** Begin by looking at which friendships, or relationships, have started to lose steam. Are you trying to hold on to any of them? If

so, how are you holding on, and what does it feel like?

2. **Let life decide.** Bring your attention to your heart and notice what feels right. The message will be uplifting and gentle, while your mind often wants to aggressively "make progress." You never know how your friendships will turn out. Friendships can come and go in cycles, where you go back and forth from everyday to nothing for years.

3. **Tap into your inner wisdom.** In the end, it comes down to listening to your heart. Are you noticing a repeating pattern in this book? Some may find this repetition boring, but the sooner you realize that listening to YOUR heart is what will lead you to a fulfilling life, the better off you will be. This is not a book about giving you one-size-fits-all tips. This book is about pointing you to your inner wisdom and true power, because that is where true change happens.

Day 17: Evolve Your Relationships

While I have an amazing relationship with my partner, Ingela, I'm not going to lie and say that it's perfect, because no relationship is.

Relationships are teachers, so sometimes Ingela and I are annoyed with each other, but we know that it's normal. We try to communicate as best as we can, and we're still learning.

Every relationship in your life has something to teach you. This doesn't mean you should never leave anyone. Sometimes what you need to learn is when to say goodbye. You'll often know what you need to learn from a relationship by looking at what you wish you could change about someone.

For example, Ingela and I sometimes disagree on how things should be cleaned. She likes to clean everything all at once, while I like to keep things clean all the time, meaning I like ongoing cleaning. At first, I wanted to change this about her. And to be honest, I still sometimes do. But as time has passed, I've started to accept it. I've realized that how things are cleaned is not as important as the relationship we have.

Another big example is the relationship I have with my son, Vincent. I don't like controlling people, and that's come to the test as my son has grown, because I have to look after him. I have to stop him from breaking things and hurting himself. I've had to learn to accept the situation, and it's helped me go deeper into the present moment, and into my heart.

So what does all of this have to do with taking your relationships to the next level? Well, it comes down to accepting people as they are. If you can't accept someone, then you may want to consider walking out the door. If you try to change someone, you expend a tremendous amount of energy, and the moment you want someone to change, even if your intentions are good, you're immediately sending the message that the person is not good as he or she is.

Immediately if I tell Ingela that she should do something my way, I'm also telling her, albeit subconsciously, that her way is wrong. And that creates friction in our relationship.

This doesn't mean we never talk about things, because we do. It has to be done gently, and all I can say is what I would prefer, and why I prefer it that way.

Opening up like this is uncomfortable, which is why most people would rather spend time complaining, arguing, and acting out. How you talk to friends will differ from how you talk to a wife or husband. But it comes down to being willing to open your heart, and realizing that your way may not always be the best way. It's just your way.

A pitfall I've had to avoid in all of my relationships is to not act when I'm in a negative state of mind. The best thing you can do is keep quiet and let the storm pass.

If you're having a bad day, and your partner has gained a few pounds, you might want to wait until your mood has passed, otherwise there may be trouble.

Evolving your relationships, both romantic and non-romantic, comes from being willing to open your heart. It won't work with everyone, because not everyone will be ready for it. But even with people who aren't willing to dive deep into their hearts with you, you can still talk to them, and understand what's going on.

Heart-Based Action Steps

In a relationship, communication is everything. The more you open up your heart, the deeper and more fulfilling your relationships will be.

Here are a few tips on how to evolve your relationships:

1. **Open your heart.** Become aware of where you protect yourself, and where you constrict around relationships. What are your biggest fears? If you aren't in a relationship right now, these questions are still relevant. You still have fears, and you still have armor around your heart.

2. **Accept.** Notice how you want to change people. Maybe you want them to be more responsible. Maybe you want them to be as into self-growth as you are. Whatever it is, let it go, and accept people as they are. You do this by noticing what feelings are inside you and by welcoming those feelings. You can be who you are, and let others be who they are. Obviously, there are exceptions, but let's stay on topic.

3. **Drop your expectations.** Just for a moment, could you let go of the expectations you have around your relationships? I know you want the best for them. But it isn't helping. It's creating more friction and more resistance. Have you noticed that when someone wants you to do something, you feel like you want to resist? That's what happens when you try to change people. The key then is to

Follow Your Heart

let go, live your life, and let people change when they want to.

Day 18: Don't Take It Personally

How would you react if someone called you fat, dumb, or incompetent? It wouldn't exactly make you happy, would it?

I used to get extremely upset if someone said anything negative to me. If I got an angry email from a customer (I run an online business), I'd feel like they were attacking me personally. Today, I realize that the anger is coming from within them. It's something they are feeling and expressing, and I just happen to be in front of them.

Don't get me wrong, I pay attention if they are pointing to something that needs to be fixed in my business, but I also don't take things personally.

We tend to walk around in life taking everything personally. If someone doesn't show up on time, we take it personally, and we start crafting a story of why they didn't show up.

As I've started relaxing my attachment to making everything personal, my life has blossomed with happiness, and my connection to my heart has deepened. This hasn't happened overnight, but over years. I still react, but I'm better than I used to be.

Let me give you an example: Years ago if I ran into someone, and they criticized me in some way, I would go into a tailspin. I could be sitting at home hours later still thinking about why they said what they said. This could go on for days, and it made me depressed. My happiness depended on what other people said. If they said something positive, I'd feel on top of the world. If they criticized me, I felt unworthy and miserable.

So how do you avoid taking things personally? For me it started with noticing what reactions I had after my initial reaction. If I get a nasty email today, I still have an emotional reaction, and I immediately start paying attention to what happens after that. I notice the stories I want to start telling myself, and just by being aware of what goes on, I calm down. It also helps me turn the spotlight on the other person, because in order for them express what they did, they must be suffering on some level.

Unfortunately, there's no quick fix. You need to uncover your patterns, and your strategies for taking things personally. You don't need to document the inner workings of your mind, you just have to become more aware of what goes on.

Avoid trying to get rid of your reactions completely, because it won't happen. You'll never achieve perfection. Wanting to be perfect is another pattern you need to be aware of.

In summary, notice how you take things personally. Also notice how nothing is truly personal. When you feel angry, you may want to express that anger. We all have our own ways of coping. For some people it may mean sending out angry emails, while others may go for a run.

Heart-Based Action Steps

Letting go of taking things personally will bring more peace and happiness to your life. It will relieve you of one more burden, and that means you'll be able to connect to your heart even better.

Here's how you can start letting go of the personal:

1. **Shift focus.** Instead of thinking about you, turn the spotlight on other people. If someone is rude to you, instead of dwelling on how rude they are, focus on what they must feel to say that. Bring your attention to your heart and wish them well (silently).

2. **Recognize our similarities.** You may not catch yourself right away, and that's okay. What matters is that you recognize and increase your awareness. Think about a time in the past when you lashed out on someone. How did you feel at that time? Why were you feeling that way? Did you end up regretting what you said? Remember we're all the same deep down. We have the same fears and dreams. When life seemingly goes against us, we become anxious and afraid. We take it out on the people around us. Wherever people express negativity, there is pain and suffering.

3. **Compassion.** Today, instead of closing down when people are hostile, open up instead. Remember where that hostility is coming from. If your partner is angry toward you, don't take it personally, but wish her well. You don't have to try to solve her problems, or make her feel better, but instead hold a space of acceptance and openness. This energy alone will affect the people around you without them even knowing it.

Day 19: Allow Abundance

In the first chapter, I shared how I used my heart to find the right house, and I want to expand on that here, because in a way, I allowed that house to come to me. When you read about abundance today, it's often about attracting, and getting, which is fine, but I like to see it more as allowing. It's a more relaxed approach.

Allowing abundance means following your heart, but also being willing to face your fears, and knowing that you are worthy of success, and whatever else you may need to fulfill your purpose. The focus is on following your heart, instead of getting money, cars, fame, and so on.

Instead of a superficial desire, you're tapping into your purpose. You're contributing to the world, and you're being provided what you need to fulfill your purpose.

The problem with superficial desires is that they often come from fear. If someone wants a lot of money, there's a good chance it comes from a place of insecurity, fear of failure, not being liked, or any of the basic fears we all have.

In our case, we needed a house, because our family was growing. For almost a year, we had needed a bigger place, but I had let my fears hold me back. I worried about how things would work out financially. I don't regret taking the extra time, because buying the house happened when I was ready.

In order to allow the house into our lives, we began by getting clear on what we wanted in a house. Ingela

Follow Your Heart

and I spoke about what we'd be willing to sacrifice, and what our priorities were. Once we were done, we let it go, and I started listening to my heart.

The first nudge I got from my heart was to start looking at houses, so I rang up a few realtors, and we began looking at what was available.

We looked for our house in a relaxed manner, hence the word allow. We didn't rush, and we didn't feel like we had to buy a house right away. We knew we'd find the right one eventually, and we did.

Allowing works on anything in life. Size doesn't matter. It could be a house, a car, or even a plot twist in your new novel. It all starts by getting clear on what you want or need, and then letting it go. Once you've let it go, start following the nudges from your heart. These nudges could be feelings, insights, inspirations, or even coincidences. The key is to not force progress, but allow it to come.

You'll also run into internal blocks to allowing abundance into your life. If you think money is evil, then you'll probably have a hard time allowing a lot of money into your life. There are many variables at play here. It's not something you have to figure out, but simply be aware of.

And if you're anything like me, the pitfall you'll repeatedly fall into is trying to force progress. When we had been looking for a house for a few months, I got impatient, and surprise surprise, I ended up frustrated and anxious. Once I realized what was going on, I took a step back, did some deep breathing, and calmed down.

Life is much easier when you realize that you don't have to go after fame, money, success, or stuff in general. You can follow your heart. You don't have to try to satisfy your fears, or live life according to other people. All you have to do is follow your heart, be clear about where you're going after, and let it come to you.

Heart-Based Action Steps

One of the best ways to allow abundance into your life is to tap into your heart. This is about looking beyond superficial desires, which usually come from other people. You learn what you "should" want, and you forget all about what you truly want.

But enough talk, here are three tips on getting this process started in your life:

1. **Get clear.** Figure out what you want. Get specific. You have to give your inner GPS the final destination. This works well for specific things like a house, but may not work for "becoming a writer." In those cases, you'll need to set a general direction, and then move onto the next step.

2. **Follow the clues.** Once you've set the final, or general, destination, it's time to follow your inner GPS. Listen to the nudges of your heart. What feels right? What feels magnetic? Go there and focus on taking one step at a time.

3. **Don't cling to any particular outcome.** Be open to whatever comes your way. The way most people try to become more abundant is by pushing, forcing, and getting. To me, that takes too much energy, so I allow things to come to me.

Day 20: Take the First Step

I haven't always done work I love. For many years, I waited. I waited for my fears to go away. I waited for something to happen. I waited until I knew more. I waited until I had more money. I was afraid of this and that. I had my reasons for why I couldn't do what made my heart sing. Until one day I became so sick of my excuses that I decided to start anyway. I didn't care if I failed, or if people laughed at me. I couldn't stand holding myself back anymore, so I took the first step.

Those early steps have led me to where I am today, helping thousands through my blog, my books, and my courses. I never knew I would end up where I am today, but I'm glad I took that first step.

I'm not saying this to brag, but to show you that you can do this, too. You can follow your heart. I don't have special talents, or powers. I'm simply a bit more stubborn than most.

As we approach the end of this book, I want to urge you to follow your heart, even if you're afraid, even if you're confused, and even if you feel overwhelmed. All you have to do is take one step at a time. You don't have to figure anything out. You simply have to start.

When you are bold enough to start, the universe will move with you. You'll experience synchronicity and serendipity. But nothing happens until you move.

You could stay put, but that's not why you're reading these words right now. Deep down, you know you need to make a change. The good news is that the change doesn't have to be big. You don't have to overhaul your whole life. All you have to do is take one tiny step. Just one.

I know it's tough to get started. It's tough to listen to your heart, because you're not sure it's going to take you where you want to go. If you're anything like me, you'll try everything else before you start trusting your heart.

Once I stopped resisting life, and began going with the flow, I breathed a sigh of relief. I still have challenges, but I realize now that I can only live life one moment at a time.

Life is an amazing mystery. You never know where it will take you. You have no idea if a negative today turns into a blessing tomorrow.

You can't predict the future. All you can do is follow your heart, and use your common sense. There's nothing magical about following your heart, yet there is. Once you start living a heart-based life, you'll know exactly what I'm talking about.

Whatever your heart is nudging you to do, do it. Take the first step. Let go of where you think it may lead. Instead of trying to anticipate what will happen, take that first step, and see what happens.

Heart-Based Action Steps

If you want more fulfillment, purpose, and happiness in your life, you have to be willing to take the first step. Nothing will happen until you do.

Here are three tips to help you get started:

1. **Follow your joy.** Most of the steps in this book begin by listening to your heart, and this one is no different. Your heart is connected to everything,

because on a molecular level, you and I, and everything else, are intertwined. When we live our lives, everything seems separate, but your heart doesn't see the world like that. This is why synchronicity is commonplace when you live from your heart.

2. **Easy does it.** You don't have to figure out where you're going. All you have to do is take one step at a time. You can use your mind, but default to listening to your heart. Your mind is a servant to your heart. When you run into frustration, take a step back, relax, and rest.

3. **Beware of big thinking.** You know you're thinking too big when you feel overwhelmed, scared, and lost. When that happens, bring your focus back to the present moment, and focus on taking one step at a time. Remember when we talked about the fog? That's what this is like. You may not see what's coming, but as you keep moving forward, you'll see where you need to go next.

Day 21: Let Go

Ten years ago, I was the epitome of someone who tried to control life. I was attached to every outcome. I thought I knew where my life was going, and what different events meant for my future. But in reality, I didn't know anything. I see that now.

This last chapter is all about letting go. It's about letting go of who you think you have to be, or what you think you have to achieve. You don't need to do anything to be happy. This doesn't mean you sit on your couch and watch movies all day long.

The letting go I'm talking about comes from releasing your grip on something you've never had any control over—your future. This book has been all about following your heart. I've shared some of my biggest realizations and biggest lessons. I don't want you to blindly believe what you've read. I want you to experiment, and to uncover what works for you, because it isn't until you apply what you've learned that you will tap into your inner power.

Letting go of trying to control doesn't mean you have no preferences. It means you become aware of the fact that you may not always know what's best for you.

It is often from the negative events in life that we grow the most. It is through suffering that we're propelled to look inside, and change.

To make this concrete, let me give you an example: When I used to worry about money, it used to pull me in. I'd end up exhausting myself by trying to come up with solutions for problems that didn't even exist. Today, I notice the worry, and I do my best to stay in the present moment. If there's something I can do, I do it. But I welcome the worry, I center myself in my heart, and I let go.

This doesn't mean that I dismiss reality. I still have to pay my bills, and I still have to do things I don't always want to do. So this is about realizing that you don't need to constantly figure things out. You can let go, and you can still take care of the practical matters of life, but just in a more relaxed, joyful way.

As you've learned in this book, I'm still learning, just like you. I don't think we'll ever stop learning, so we might as well accept that we'll bump into challenges for as long as we live. The key then is not to try and get rid of all of our problems and challenges, but to learn to accept them as a part of life.

Don't look at letting go as another task you have to accomplish. Keep it in mind as you go about your day, and do your best to not get involved in your thoughts. Remember that you do not have to rush to become someone, or to accomplish anything, in order to be fulfilled.

Your heart knows what's right for you, and what's not. Other people can give you advice, but ultimately you have to discover if that advice feels true.

Letting go is not easy. In fact, most people will avoid it at all costs, because they believe they are in complete control of their lives. And while you do have the power to choose, you have to admit that you can't ultimately control, or figure out, life.

And you know what? You won't let go, not at first. And that's okay. Don't criticize yourself over it. Just be with it and let go of what you let go of. Let the rest be.

Heart-Based Action Steps

Peace is not something that is given to you when your life is perfect, it's what is always inside of you. It is who you are deep down.
   Here are three tips on how to play with letting go:

1. **Stop trying so hard.** We're told we have to work hard and figure everything out. We have to be in control. But what if we don't? What if we can let life unfold naturally? I'm not saying you have to live like this for the rest of your life. I'm merely suggesting that you try it out for one day. For one day, stop trying so hard, and notice what happens.

2. **Trust your heart.** When you trust your heart, you realize that you don't have to try so hard. You don't have to know what's coming. You feel happier, and you're more fulfilled. That's what everyone wants, and it's all right there, inside your heart. Today, revel in your heart, and what it's telling you.

3. **Enjoy.** In the end, life comes down to enjoying the present moment. You don't have to wait for anything. You don't even have to wait to follow your heart. You can start enjoying life right now. Enjoy your friends, family, or whatever is in your life. Give yourself a day of joy. You've earned it.

Conclusion

You've come to the end of the book. Whether or not you worked through one chapter per day doesn't matter. What matters is that you take what you've learned to heart and use it in your life. If you're skeptical, that's good, because it means that you don't believe everything you're told. But don't take it too far. Instead, experiment with what you've learned, and find out for yourself if it works or not.

As you've noticed, many of the chapters had overlapping lessons, but they approached the core theme from different angles, which will help cement what you've learned. This whole book comes down to one thing: following your heart.

To help you refresh your memory, here are the three core elements of living a heart-based life:

1. **Listen.** You start by listening to what your heart is telling you. Where is it pulling you? What feels magnetic? When you're starting out, you may not know how your heart communicates. If so, you pretend you know. Make a game of it. Make it playful.

2. **Move.** Then you take the next step. You follow the nudges of your heart as best you can, while including your mind, and respecting your fears. You realize that you don't have to figure life out in order to move forward. You only have to worry

about taking one tiny step at a time, and listen to your heart.

3. **Welcome.** Once in a while, stop and welcome any fears, discomfort, and anxiety. Notice when you run into frustration, and when you try too hard. Welcome these feelings. Don't push them away, but let them be in your body.

Learning to follow your heart is not easy. It's often a struggle at first when you learn to give control to your heart. Your mind will not want to give up control, because it still falsely believes that it has control over life. It believes that if it could just figure things out, everything would be okay.

But the truth is that everything is okay right now. Life is evolving in the way it should. You may not like hearing this, but remember, I'm not here to tell you how to live your life or what to believe. I'm here to share how I view the world and how I live from my heart.

I hope you take from this book what resonates with you, because that is the first step in following your heart. I don't expect everything to have been a good fit for you, but if you've taken even a few things out of this book, that's enough.

Feel free to return to the chapters that most resonated with you. Build on them, and experiment. Instead of doing each chapter for a day, do one chapter for a week, or even a month. And when you feel ready, let go of this book, and simply listen to your heart, because that is where you will find true fulfillment and happiness.

Thank You

Before I let you go, I'd like to thank you for taking the time to read this book. I appreciate it. If you have any questions, or would like to share your progress, I'm always one email away at henri@wakeupcloud.com.

I see all emails and try to reply to them as soon as I can. If you don't hear from me within 72 hours, please email me again because chances are that your email got lost in cyberspace.

I'd also like to ask that if you liked this book, and got something out of it, that you leave a review on Amazon, because it'll help this message reach more people and help them listen to their hearts. And in the end, that is how we will change the world: one person at a time.

Thank you for being awesome.

Connect

If you'd like to learn more about me, you can find me on:

My website: http://www.wakeupcloud.com/
Twitter: http://www.twitter.com/henrijunttila
Facebook: https://www.facebook.com/WakeUpCloud

And as I mentioned earlier, if you have any questions, comments, or just want to say hi, feel free to email me at henri@wakeupcloud.com.

The Next Step

You've just read *Follow Your Heart: 21 Days to a Happier, More Fulfilling Life*, where you learned to tap into your inner GPS.

But do you know what you're passionate about? That may take some extra exploration, which is why I wrote a book called: *Find Your Passion: 25 Questions You Must Ask Yourself*. This book will not give you the cookie cutter advice you've heard before. It will give you the questions that allow you to uncover your true passions.

These two books go hand in hand. They complement each other to help you dive deeper into living a life full of purpose, joy, and fulfillment.

If you're interested in learning more, you can find the book (and all my other books) at Amazon.com. Just search for my name "Henri Junttila."

Printed in Great Britain
by Amazon